MW01153268

FREEDOM'S PROMISE

LOVING V.
VIRGINIA

BY DUCHESS HARRIS, JD, PHD
WITH MARNE VENTURA

Core Library

An Imprint of Abdo Publishing
abdobooks.com

Cover image: Mildred Loving, *left*, and Richard Loving,
right, fought in court for their right to marry.

abdocorelibrary.com

Published by Abdo Publishing, a division of ABDO, PO Box 398166,
Minneapolis, Minnesota 55439. Copyright © 2020 by Abdo Consulting
Group, Inc. International copyrights reserved in all countries. No part of this
book may be reproduced in any form without written permission from the
publisher. Core Library™ is a trademark and logo of Abdo Publishing.

Printed in the United States of America, North Mankato, Minnesota
012019
092019

**THIS BOOK CONTAINS
RECYCLED MATERIALS**

Cover Photo: Francis Miller/The Life Picture Collection/Getty Images
Interior Photos: Francis Miller/The Life Picture Collection/Getty Images, 1; Bettmann/Getty
Images, 5, 26–27; AP Images, 6–7; North Wind Picture Archives, 11; Francisco Macías/Library
of Congress, 12; The Free Lance–Star/AP Images, 16–17, 43; John Vachon/Everett Collection/
Newscom, 19; Warren K. Leffler/Everett Collection/Newscom, 20; Red Line Editorial, 24, 38;
iStockphoto, 28; Bill O'Leary/The Washington Post/Getty Images, 31; Joe Ravi/Shutterstock Images,
34–35; Mike Morones/The Free Lance–Star/AP Images, 37; Robert A. Martin/The Free Lance–Star/
AP Images, 40

Editor: Maddie Spalding
Series Designer: Claire Vanden Branden

Library of Congress Control Number: 2018964503

Publisher's Cataloging-in-Publication Data

Names: Harris, Duchess, author | Ventura, Marne, author.
Title: Loving v. Virginia / by Duchess Harris and Marne Ventura
Description: Minneapolis, Minnesota : Abdo Publishing, 2020 | Series: Freedom's promise |
    Includes online resources and index.
Identifiers: ISBN 9781532118777 (lib. bdg.) | ISBN 9781532172953 (ebook)
Subjects: LCSH: Interracial marriage--Law and legislation--Juvenile literature. | Loving,
    Mildred Jeter--Juvenile literature. | Loving, Richard Perry--Juvenile literature. | United
    States. Constitution. 14th Amendment--Juvenile literature. | Racism--United States--
    History--20th century--Juvenile literature.
Classification: DDC 346.7301--dc23

CONTENTS

A LETTER FROM DUCHESS

In 1961 Ann Dunham got married in Hawaii. Dunham was a white woman. She married a man from Kenya. The marriage was legal in Hawaii. But some states outlawed interracial marriage then. Dunham later gave birth to Barack Obama, future US president.

Three years earlier, another interracial couple had also married. Their names were Richard and Mildred Loving. They were arrested in Virginia for breaking the state's interracial marriage laws. The judge gave them a choice: They could go to jail for one year or leave Virginia. They chose to leave the state. But they later brought their case to court. In 1967 the Lovings won a case in the US Supreme Court. The court's ruling struck down interracial marriage bans throughout the country.

This book explores the lives and legacy of the Lovings. Join me on a journey that tells the story of the promise of love and the promise of freedom.

Duchess Harris

Mildred Loving, *left,* **and Richard Loving,** *right,* **were arrested just weeks after they married.**

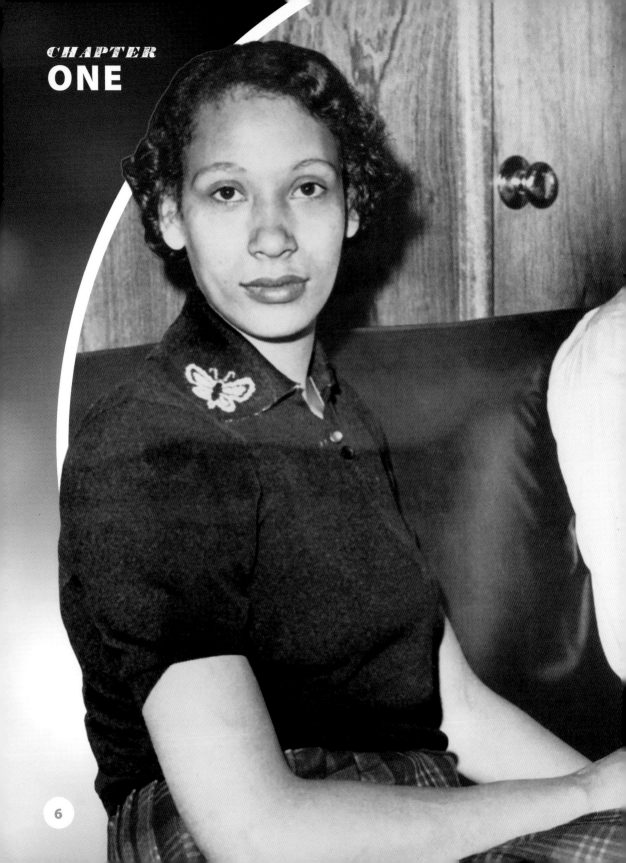

MR. AND MRS. LOVING

Newlyweds Richard and Mildred Loving lay asleep in bed. At two o'clock in the morning, they awoke to loud knocking. The door burst open. A sheriff and two deputies rushed in. The sheriff pointed a flashlight at their faces.

The sheriff asked Richard what he was doing in bed with Mildred. Mildred pointed at their marriage license on the dresser. She explained that she was his wife. The sheriff replied that the couple could not be husband and wife in Virginia.

The date was July 11, 1958. The place was Central Point, Virginia. The officers had been

Mildred and Richard Loving married in 1958.

sent by the county attorney to arrest the Lovings. The attorney had received an anonymous tip that Richard and Mildred had broken a state law. The law banned interracial marriage.

Twenty-five-year-old Richard was a white construction worker. Nineteen-year-old Mildred was of mixed African American and Native American descent. The two were longtime friends. They were in love. Five weeks ago, they had traveled to Washington, DC. Interracial marriage was legal there. They married and returned to their hometown. They were staying in the downstairs bedroom of Mildred's parents' house while Richard built them a home of their own. Mildred was pregnant with their first child.

INTERRACIAL MARRIAGE LAWS

In 1958 marriage between white and black people was illegal in Virginia and 23 other US states. These laws had been in place for many years. Virginia's first law banning interracial marriage was passed in 1691. At that time,

Virginia was a colony. Virginia law forbade white people from marrying black people and Native Americans. The punishment for breaking this law was banishment from the colony. In 1705 Virginia's lawmakers changed the punishment. Any white person who married a black person would be jailed and forced to pay a fine. The minister who performed the wedding ceremony would be fined too.

Other laws in the colonies made it illegal for black and white people to have children together. Still, slaveholders sometimes had children with the women they enslaved. By law, the child of an enslaved woman would also be a slave. The child would

JUMPING THE BROOM

Enslaved people were not allowed to be married in an official ceremony. Instead, enslaved couples were often married in a ceremony called jumping the broom. A broom was laid on the ground or held in the air. The couple jumped over the broom. This ceremony symbolized the sweeping away of evil spirits. It recognized the couple as husband and wife.

be enslaved under the same slaveholder as the mother. In this way, the slaveholder would gain more slaves.

In 1705 Virginia lawmakers defined different racial groups. They said that black people and Native Americans could be legally enslaved. They also defined some people as "mulattoes." Anyone who was the child of a Native American was considered a mulatto. Anyone who was the child, grandchild, or great-grandchild of a black person was considered a mulatto. Virginia law said that mulattoes could be enslaved too. Lawmakers used these classifications to restrict certain people's rights. The laws they created were called slave codes.

In 1924 Virginia passed the Racial Integrity Act. The purpose of this act was to stop white people from marrying and having children with people of other races. This law was based on the belief that white people are better than others. Many white people thought that marrying people of other races would taint the white race. The punishment for interracial marriage

Settlers first brought enslaved Africans to the Jamestown colony in Virginia in the 1600s.

was one to five years in jail. This punishment applied to both the husband and wife.

The Racial Integrity Act defined a white person as someone with light skin who had European ancestry. These people were called Caucasians. The act defined

VIRGINIA

HEALTH BULLETIN

| Vol. XVI. | MARCH, 1924. | Extra No. 2 |

Virginia's Racial Integrity Act outlawed marriage between white people and people of other races.

The New Virginia Law
To Preserve Racial Integrity

W. A. PLECKER, M. D., *State Registrar of Vital Statistics, Richmond, Va.*

Senate Bill 219, To preserve racial integrity, passed the House March 8, 1924, and is now a law of the State.

This bill aims at correcting a condition which only the more thoughtful people of Virginia know the existence of.

It is estimated that there are in the State from 10,000 to 20,000, possibly more, near white people, who are known to possess an intermixture of colored blood, in some cases to a slight extent it is true, but still enough to prevent them from being white.

In the past it has been possible for these people to declare themselves as white, or even to have the Court so declare them. Then they have demanded the admittance of their children into the white schools, and in not a few cases have intermarried with white people.

In many counties they exist as distinct colonies holding themselves aloof from negroes, but not being admitted by the white people as of their race.

In any large gathering or school of colored people, especially in the cities, many will be observed who are scarcely distinguishable as colored.

These persons, however, are not white in reality, nor by the new definition of this law, that a white person is one with no trace of the blood of another race, except that a person with one-sixteenth of the

certain other people as colored based on their ancestry. This term was used for anyone who had one-sixteenth or more African American ancestry. Anyone who had one-sixteenth or more Native American ancestry was considered Native American.

TOUGH CHOICES

After they were arrested, Richard and Mildred were put in a nearby jail. Richard was released after one night. Mildred was released a few days later.

In October the local court formally accused Richard and Mildred of breaking the law. Their first court hearing was in January 1959. They at first pleaded not guilty. But they changed their plea by the end of the hearing. The judge had given them a choice. They faced a year in jail as punishment for breaking the Racial Integrity Act. But if they pled guilty, they would not be sentenced to any jail time. Instead they would both have to leave the state. They could not return to Virginia together for 25 years. Richard and Mildred did not want to leave their home. But they did not want to go to jail either. They agreed to the deal.

The Lovings wanted to live together in their hometown. But they did not have this freedom. In a few years, they would begin a series of court cases that would change the lives of interracial couples in the United States.

STRAIGHT TO THE
SOURCE

The Racial Integrity Act outlawed interracial marriage. It defined people as white, colored, or American Indian based on their ancestry. It said:

> If there is reasonable cause to disbelieve that applicants are of pure white race, . . . the clerk or deputy clerk shall withhold the granting of the license until satisfactory proof is produced that both applicants are "white persons" as provided for in this act. . . . It shall thereafter be unlawful for any white person in this State to marry any save a white person, or a person with no other admixture of blood than white and American Indian. For the purpose of this act, the term "white person" shall apply only to the person who has no trace whatsoever of any blood other than Caucasian; but persons who have one-sixteenth or less of the blood of the American Indian and have no other non-Caucasic blood shall be deemed to be white persons.

Source: "An Act to Preserve Racial Integrity." *Virginia Center for Digital History*. Virginia Center for Digital History, n.d. Web. Accessed October 12, 2018.

What's the Big Idea?

Take a close look at this passage. How did the Racial Integrity Act define a white person? What language shows how the act discriminated against nonwhite people?

FIGHTING FOR JUSTICE

In the mid-1900s, interracial marriage bans were part of a wider pattern of racist laws in the United States. The Thirteenth Amendment had ended slavery in 1865. But southern lawmakers found ways to deny black people rights. They passed the first Jim Crow laws in the 1870s. Jim Crow laws made racial segregation legal. Racial segregation is the forced separation of people based on race. Black people were discriminated against because of their race. They could not attend the same schools as white people. They had to use separate public transportation and facilities. These laws were meant to keep black

The Lovings wanted to be able to live together as a family in Virginia.

people from interacting with white people. Many Jim Crow laws were still in force in the mid-1900s.

After their hearing in 1959, the Lovings each had to pay court fees. They moved in with Mildred's cousin in Washington, DC. Richard found work as a bricklayer.

By 1963 the Lovings had two sons and one daughter. Mildred and Richard had each gone back to visit Central Point. But their court sentence forbade them from returning together. Mildred had returned to Central Point for the births of their daughter and younger son. Mildred's family lived in Central Point. She wanted her family to be near when her children were born.

Mildred and Richard missed their friends and family in Virginia. They had trouble earning enough money to pay their bills. They wanted to go home together with their children.

Jim Crow laws forced black people to use separate facilities, such as water fountains.

THE CIVIL RIGHTS MOVEMENT

In the 1950s and 1960s, many people protested racist laws across the country. This struggle is called the American civil rights movement. A major event in the movement took place on August 28, 1963. Approximately 250,000 people marched in

Thousands of people participated in the March on Washington for Jobs and Freedom in 1963.

Washington, DC. This march was called the March on Washington for Jobs and Freedom. The purpose of the march was to protest the unfair treatment of African Americans. Black people were discriminated against in many ways. They often had a hard time getting jobs. Some employers would not hire them because they were African American. The police also discriminated against African Americans. Police officers often used violence against black people.

Protesters at the March on Washington asked for an end to school segregation. They also asked for an end to police violence. They asked for programs to help black people get jobs.

Mildred's cousin gave her an idea. He suggested that Mildred follow the protesters' example. He said she should fight for her right to return home, just as the protesters were fighting for their rights. Mildred agreed. She wrote a letter to US Attorney General Robert F. Kennedy.

PERSPECTIVES
MILDRED LOVING

The civil rights movement was in full swing when Mildred asked Robert Kennedy for help. Some people believe the Lovings were civil rights activists. But Mildred later said that their goal was not to further the cause of civil rights. She said they were just trying to get back home to Virginia.

Mildred explained that she and Richard wanted to be able to return to Virginia as a family.

ROBERT F. KENNEDY

Robert F. Kennedy was the brother of John F. Kennedy. John was president of the United States from 1961 to 1963. John appointed Robert as attorney general. Robert served as attorney general from 1961 to 1964. Both Robert and John supported the civil rights movement. In 1962 the US Supreme Court ordered the admission of the first black student to the University of Mississippi. Robert sent federal troops to Mississippi to make sure the order was enforced.

THE ACLU TAKES THEIR CASE

Kennedy read Mildred's letter. He wrote back. He told her to contact the American Civil Liberties Union (ACLU). The ACLU's mission is to make sure all US citizens are treated fairly.

The ACLU agreed to take the Lovings' case. ACLU lawyer Bernard Cohen began work in June 1963. Lawyer Philip Hirschkop joined the team a few months later.

BAZILE'S DECISION

Virginia law said that appeals must be made within 60 days of a judge's ruling. An appeal is a request for the court to reconsider a ruling. Judges can overturn a previous ruling in an appeals trial. Cohen asked Leon Bazile to let the Lovings file an appeal in November 1963. Bazile had found the Lovings guilty in their initial trial. More than four years had passed since then. Still, Bazile let the Lovings file an appeal.

Bazile presided over the Lovings' appeals trial. He did not change his ruling. He found the Lovings guilty again on January 22, 1965. He said that they had committed a serious crime. He argued that the law was needed to keep social order. Bazile believed that interracial couples that married should be punished. He said that it did not matter if their wedding was legal in Washington, DC. In Virginia, it was not. He believed that if he let people break Virginia law based on laws in other states, it would weaken laws in Virginia.

ANTI-MISCEGENATION
LAWS

Laws against interracial marriages were called anti-miscegenation laws. The below map shows the states that had these laws. It also shows the years in which these laws were repealed. The white states did not have anti-miscegenation laws in the 1900s. Why do you think the purple states were the last to repeal these laws?

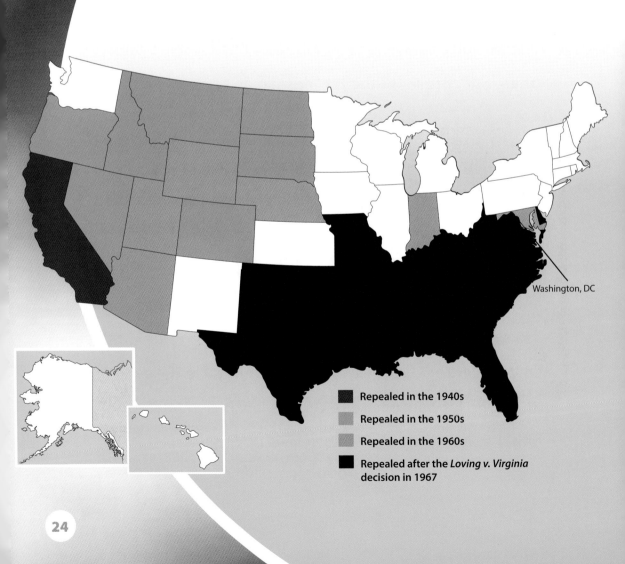

Washington, DC

■ Repealed in the 1940s

■ Repealed in the 1950s

■ Repealed in the 1960s

■ Repealed after the *Loving v. Virginia* decision in 1967

The Lovings were disappointed. They still could not live together as a family in their hometown. But their lawyers told them they could keep fighting. They could file an appeal with a higher court. Bazile's ruling made it clear that he believed black people were not equal to white people. His ruling was a form of racial discrimination. The lawyers wanted to use this argument at their next appeal. The Lovings decided to take their case to the Supreme Court of Virginia.

EXPLORE ONLINE

Chapter Two talks about the civil rights movement. The article at the website below goes into more depth on this topic. How is the information from the website the same as the information in Chapter Two? What new information did you learn from the website?

THE CIVIL RIGHTS MOVEMENT
abdocorelibrary.com/loving-v-virginia

AN UPHILL BATTLE

Before the Lovings' case, other interracial couples had tried to fight interracial marriage bans. In 1878 Andrew and Mahala Kinney married in Washington, DC. Andrew was a black man. Mahala was a white woman. They returned to their home in Virginia and were arrested. They were found guilty in a lower court. They appealed their case to the Supreme Court of Virginia. The court upheld their convictions. The judge ruled that Virginia state law could override the laws of another state. The Kinneys were allowed to live together as husband and wife in Virginia. But they had to pay fines.

Lawyer Philip Hirschkop, *center*, **helped defend the Lovings in court in the 1960s.**

The Supreme Court of Virginia reviews decisions made by lower courts within the state.

An 1883 case called *Pace v. Alabama* also involved an interracial couple. Tony Pace was a black man. He had married Mary Cox, a white woman. They wanted to file an appeal with the US Supreme Court. Their marriage had been ruled illegal in Alabama. The Supreme Court would not take their case. The court ruled that because the punishment in Alabama was the same for both white and black partners, the law was fair. The court said the law did not violate the Fourteenth Amendment. The Fourteenth Amendment gives all US citizens equal protection under the law.

In 1888 the US Supreme Court took a case called *Maynard v. Hill*. This case was not about interracial marriage. The people involved in the case were David and Lydia Maynard. David and Lydia were both white. The case was about states' rights.

PLESSY V. FERGUSON

In 1896 the Supreme Court ruled in a case called *Plessy v. Ferguson*. It found that racial segregation did not violate the Constitution. The ruling said that segregation was legal as long as the same services were provided to both black and white people. But in reality, the services provided to black people were often worse than those provided to white people. For example, schools for black children often did not have enough supplies. They did not get enough funding.

David and Lydia had married in Vermont in 1828. They moved to Ohio with their children in 1850. Then David left the family and moved to Oregon. He divorced Lydia. He married another woman. Lydia did not agree to the divorce. But the state of Oregon said David's new marriage was legal. The Supreme Court ruled that states had the right to declare a marriage legal or illegal. A state did not have to accept a marriage that had been declared legal in another state.

THE SUPREME COURT OF VIRGINIA

On March 7, 1966, the Supreme Court of Virginia ruled on the Lovings' appeal. The judge found the Lovings guilty of breaking the Racial Integrity Act. But he said that preventing Mildred and Richard from living together within the state for 25 years was not reasonable. He said that the judge should have followed the law and sentenced the couple to one to five years in jail.

Mildred Loving wrote letters to lawyer Philip Hirschkop when the Lovings needed his advice.

April 5, 1967
Helmet, Va.

Dear Mr. Hirschkop,
  We recieved your
letter and are very happy
to know about the trail
of April 10th.
    We would love to
come if we could be
of any help, but other-
wise, we wouldn't
understand anything,
and would be nervous.
    Do you have any idea
when a decision will be
made?
    If we can be of any
help let us know.

Daniel J. DeMarco

DJD/pam

PERSPECTIVES

SCHOOL SEGREGATION

In 1954 the US Supreme Court ruled on a case called *Brown v. Board of Education of Topeka*. The court said that school segregation violated the Fourteenth Amendment. This ruling paved the way for school desegregation. White schools around the country began admitting black students. Some lawyers had argued in favor of segregated schools. The Constitution did not say that white and black children had to go to the same schools. Lawyers used this fact to make their arguments. They also claimed that segregation did not harm black people. They also claimed that white people were trying to provide black people with equally good schools.

The Lovings were not imprisoned. But they were back where they had started. The Supreme Court of Virginia had upheld Virginia's interracial marriage laws. Still, the Lovings decided to keep fighting. They asked the US Supreme Court to hear their case. To their surprise, the court agreed.

STRAIGHT TO THE
SOURCE

In a 2007 interview with National Public Radio, lawyer Bernard Cohen talked about the Lovings' case. He said:

> *They [the Lovings] were very simple people, who were not interested in winning any civil rights principle. They just were in love with one another and wanted the right to live together as husband and wife in Virginia, without any interference. . . . When I told Richard [Loving] that this case was, in all likelihood, going to go to the Supreme Court of the United States, he became wide-eyed and his jaw dropped.*

> Source: "Loving Decision: 40 Years of Legal Interracial Unions." *National Public Radio*. National Public Radio, June 11, 2007. Web. Accessed October 12, 2018.

Consider Your Audience

Adapt this passage for a different audience, such as your friends. Write a blog post conveying this same information for the new audience. How does your post differ from the original text and why?

A HISTORIC DECISION

I n April 1967, the case of *Loving v. Virginia* was brought to the US Supreme Court. The Lovings' lawyers used the *Brown v. Board of Education of Topeka* ruling to support their argument. The *Brown* ruling set a precedent for the Lovings' case. A precedent is a court ruling that can be used in later court cases. The *Brown* decision ended school segregation. It ruled that Jim Crow laws were not fair. The Lovings' lawyers said that interracial marriage laws were also not fair.

The Civil Rights Act also helped the Lovings. President John F. Kennedy had first proposed this act. President Lyndon B. Johnson

The US Supreme Court is the highest court in the United States.

RICHARD LOVING

Cohen made a strong argument in the *Loving v. Virginia* case. He said that all US citizens have the right to be treated equally by the court system. He referred to the Constitution and the Fourteenth Amendment. But he told the court that Richard Loving had the best argument. Richard and Mildred chose not to attend the hearing because they did not like being in public. Cohen had asked Richard if he had any message to deliver to the court. Richard had simply said, "Tell the Court I love my wife and it is just not fair that I can't live with her in Virginia."

signed it into law in 1964. The act ended segregation in public places. It banned job discrimination based on race. The Lovings' lawyers argued that interracial marriage bans were also a form of racial discrimination.

The nine Supreme Court justices heard arguments from both sides. On June 12, 1967, the justices overturned the Lovings' convictions. The justices agreed that citizens should not be denied the right to marry because of their races. Chief Justice Earl Warren said that the

The Lovings' daughter, Peggy Loving Fortune, *left*, reads a highway marker in Virginia that honors her parents. Her grandson, Mark Loving II, stands beside her.

freedom to marry is a basic civil right. All of the justices agreed that Virginia's interracial marriage ban went against the Fourteenth Amendment. Warren read the Supreme Court's ruling aloud in court. He said that no state had the right to discriminate against black people.

INTERRACIAL MARRIAGE

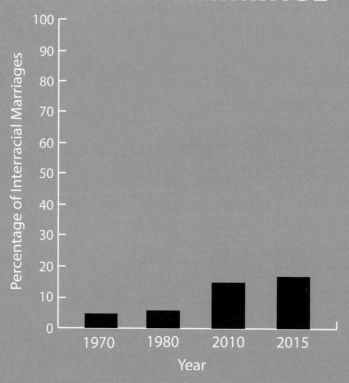

The above graph shows the percentage of interracial marriages among all marriages in the United States in certain years. How has this percentage changed over time? How do you think the *Loving v. Virginia* ruling may have influenced these changes?

At the time, 16 states still outlawed interracial marriage. The *Loving v. Virginia* ruling ended those laws. The Supreme Court confirmed that the Fourteenth Amendment gave citizenship and equal rights to African Americans. The court defended a person's right to marry a person of another race.

At last the Lovings were found not guilty. They were legally man and wife. The Lovings had been secretly living on a farm in Virginia during their appeals trial. They had been careful not to give interviews or be seen in public. They did not want anyone to discover that they were illegally living together in Virginia. But after the Supreme Court ruling, they were free to live as a family in Virginia. Richard built them a house in Central Point.

On June 29, 1975, a drunk driver ran into Richard and Mildred's car. Richard was killed. Mildred survived. But she was left blind in one eye. She died of pneumonia on May 2, 2008.

LOVING

The movie *Loving* was released in 2016. It tells the Lovings' story, including their personal lives and their court cases. It celebrates the strength of their love. The movie contrasts their loving family life with the harsh way they were treated by the legal system. Many film critics praised the movie.

After Richard's death, Mildred remained in the house he had built in Central Point.

A LASTING LEGACY

The *Loving v. Virginia* ruling changed the lives of many Americans. States had to honor the right of interracial couples to marry. The ruling was an important victory for the civil rights movement. It also set an important standard for later court cases involving marriage rights.

Loving v. Virginia has been used as a precedent to argue that choosing a marriage partner is a basic civil right. This precedent has been used to argue for the right of same-sex couples to marry.

The Lovings' determination helped change the course of history. Their legal battle helped secure marriage rights for many Americans. Each year on June 12, people celebrate the anniversary of the *Loving v. Virginia* decision. This holiday is called Loving Day.

FURTHER EVIDENCE

Chapter Four explores the *Loving v. Virginia* ruling and its legacy. What is one of the main points of this chapter? What evidence is included to support this point? Read the article at the website below. Does the information on the website support the main point of the chapter? Does it present new evidence?

LOVING V. VIRGINIA
abdocorelibrary.com/loving-v-virginia

FAST FACTS

- In 1924 Virginia passed the Racial Integrity Act. This act banned interracial marriage.

- On June 2, 1958, Mildred and Richard Loving were married in Washington, DC. Mildred was African American and Native American. Richard was white.

- The Lovings went back to Central Point, Virginia. They were arrested and tried for breaking the Racial Integrity Act. The Lovings pled guilty. The judge ruled that they could not return to Virginia together for 25 years.

- In June 1963, the ACLU helped the Lovings appeal their case. But the judge refused to overturn their convictions.

- The Lovings' case went to the Supreme Court of Virginia in 1966. The court upheld the Lovings' convictions.

- The Lovings' case went to the US Supreme Court in 1967. The court ruled that interracial marriage bans violate the US Constitution. The Lovings were found not guilty.

- The *Loving v. Virginia* decision made it possible for interracial couples around the country to marry legally. Today it remains an important precedent for civil rights cases.

STOP AND
THINK

Why Do I Care?

The *Loving v. Virginia* case happened more than 50 years ago. But that doesn't mean you can't think about its legacy. How do you think this decision affects the lives of people today?

Surprise Me

Chapter One discusses interracial marriage laws in the 1950s and 1960s. After reading this book, what two or three facts about these laws did you find most surprising? Write a few sentences about each fact. Why did you find each fact surprising?

You Are There

Chapter Four discusses how the Lovings' lawyers defended their marriage in the *Loving v. Virginia* case. Imagine you were a reporter in the courtroom. Write a newspaper article describing the case. What arguments were made? What was the reason for the ruling?

GLOSSARY

amendment
a change or an addition to an existing law

ancestry
a person's relatives from earlier generations or ethnic descent

appeal
a legal case where a higher court is asked to reconsider a ruling

colony
land owned by a faraway country or nation

conviction
a court ruling that finds a person guilty

discrimination
the unjust treatment of a person or group based on race or other perceived differences

interracial
involving people of different races

miscegenation
an offensive term for marrying or having children with a partner of a different race

repeal
to undo a law

ONLINE
RESOURCES

To learn more about *Loving v. Virginia*, visit our free resource websites below.

Visit **abdocorelibrary.com** or scan this QR code for free Common Core resources for teachers and students, including vetted activities, multimedia, and booklinks, for deeper subject comprehension.

Visit **abdobooklinks.com** or scan this QR code for free additional online weblinks for further learning. These links are routinely monitored and updated to provide the most current information available.

LEARN
MORE

Uhl, Xina M. *The Passing of the Civil Rights Act of 1964*. Minneapolis, MN: Abdo Publishing, 2016.

Winter, Max. *The Civil Rights Movement*. Minneapolis, MN: Abdo Publishing, 2015.

ABOUT THE
AUTHORS

Duchess Harris, JD, PhD

Dr. Harris is a professor of American Studies at Macalester College and curator of the Duchess Harris Collection of ABDO books. She is also the coauthor of the titles in the collection, which features popular selections such as *Hidden Human Computers: The Black Women of NASA* and series including News Literacy and Being Female in America.

Before working with ABDO, Dr. Harris authored several other books on the topics of race, culture, and American history. She served as an associate editor for *Litigation News*, the American Bar Association Section of Litigation's quarterly flagship publication, and was the first editor in chief of *Law Raza*, an interactive online journal covering race and the law, published at William Mitchell College of Law. She has earned a PhD in American Studies from the University of Minnesota and a JD from William Mitchell College of Law.

Marne Ventura

Marne Ventura has written many books for kids. A former elementary school teacher, she holds a master's degree in education from the University of California. Her favorite topics include history, science, arts, crafts, and food. Marne and her husband live in California.

INDEX